# Insects and Plants

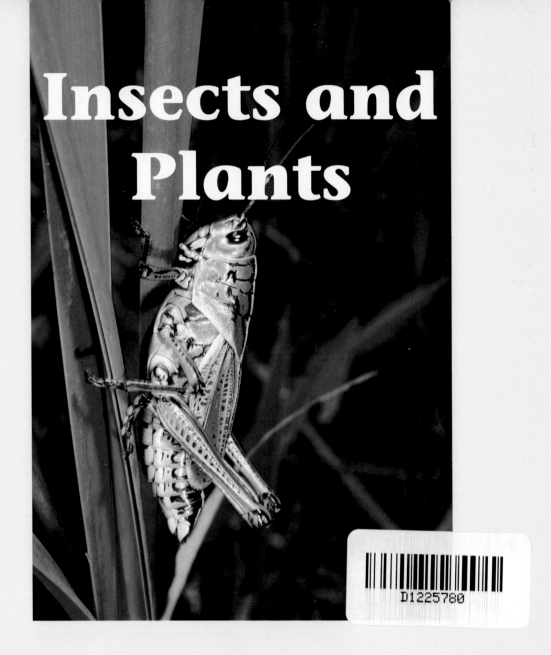

Developed at
**Lawrence Hall of Science**
University of California at Berkeley

Published and Distributed by **Delta Education**

1012457
978-1-59821-794-0
1 2 3 4 5 6 7 8 QUE 13 12 11 10 09 08

1

# Table of Contents

# So Many Kinds, So Many Places

This amazing animal is an **insect.**
Flies, ants, and crickets are all
insects, too. There are so many kinds
of insects. Insects are everywhere!
Can you name some others?

No matter where you are, there is probably an insect near you. Insects are in the air and in the water. They creep in the Arctic snow. Others scamper around in the desert.

These ladybugs have gathered on a tree trunk.
Other insects live on the tops of mountains.
Some insects live in the jungles of the rain
forest. Insects are everywhere!

Insects may seem like pests to you.
Some insects eat our clothes,
buildings, and crops. But insects
are very important. Many
different animals need them
for food.

Insects are important for people, too.
Bees visit **flowers** and that helps **fruit**
grow. They also make sweet honey.

People use the thread from
the cocoon of the silk worm
to make clothing.

# Environment

The **adult** mealworm is called a
darkling beetle. You can tell it
is an insect. It has a head with
**antennae.** It has a thorax with six
legs. And it has an abdomen. All
darkling beetles are the same.
Or are they?

If you look closely, you might see that some darkling beetles are a little different. Some are smaller. Most are black, but some are brown or tan.

Darkling beetles **inherit** most of their **characteristics** from their parents. Darkling beetles get their size and color from their parents. They get their head, antennae, thorax, and six legs from their parents.

Some darkling beetle characteristics are caused by the **environment.** Things can happen to change how a beetle looks.

If a beetle gets into a fight, it might lose a piece of wing cover. It could even lose a leg. The beetle looks different.

If the beetle becomes a parent, what will its **offspring** look like? Will they have broken wing covers and five legs? No. Changes like these are caused by the environment. They are not passed on to offspring.

Look at these trees. Why are they this shape?

These trees live in a very windy environment. The environment has shaped the trees.

What if a **seed** from a wind-shaped tree were planted in a place with no wind? The seed would grow into a tree that looks like this.

11

Acorns are the seeds of oak trees. Every year an oak tree grows acorns. Some years, the tree has hundreds of acorns. Other years, it has only a few acorns. What causes this difference?

Environment causes this difference. The tree grows lots of acorns when the environment is good. A good environment is warm. A good environment has plenty of water. It has lots of sunshine, too.

The tree grows few acorns when the environment is bad. A bad environment is too cold or too dry.

You can plant an acorn from a tree with lots of acorns. It will grow into an oak tree. Will it make lots of acorns every year? No. The new oak tree will make lots of acorns only when the environment is good. When the environment is bad, the tree will make only a few acorns.

# Environment Review

1. What can happen to a darkling beetle to change its characteristics?

2. Will these changes be passed to offspring?

3. What characteristics of a tree can the environment change?

# Flowers and Seeds

These are wild brassica plants. Each plant grows lots of flowers. But the brassica plant does not grow flowers to look pretty. The flowers are an important part of the plant's **life cycle.**

Soon the flowers fade and dry up. And something new appears right where each flower once grew. It looks like a little green bean. It is a seedpod.

Weeks later, the pods are big and dry. There are about six seeds inside each pod. What do you think will happen if someone plants the new seeds?

Brassicas aren't the only plants that make seeds. Cherry trees make seeds. Where are they found? There is one seed inside each cherry. And where does the cherry grow? It grows right where the cherry flower was.

Plants grow flowers. The flowers grow into fruit. Fruit have seeds inside. When the seeds grow into new plants, it is called **reproduction.**

A tomato is a fruit. It has seeds. Have you ever seen tomato flowers?

Can you see the strawberry flowers? Strawberry flowers grow into fruit.

New plants grow from seeds. Seeds are found in fruit. Fruit grow out of flowers. Flowers and fruit are important in the life cycles of plants.

# Flowers and Seeds Review

1. Name one of the plants, and tell about its flower.

2. Where are the seeds on a full-grown brassica plant?

3. Name two fruits you like to eat.

4. Name the parts of plants that are important for their life cycle.

19

# Variation

**Variation** means difference. When we looked at the darkling beetles, we saw variation. They were not all the same. Do other **organisms** have variation?

People are different. Some people are short. Some can run fast. Some have brown eyes. Some have black hair. Some have freckles. Everyone is different when you look close enough.

Sometimes it is hard to see variation. Black bears look very much alike. But they do have color variation. Can you see color variation in this picture?

Trout have color variation, too. Some
of them are silver. Others are brightly
colored. Some have lots of spots.
Others have only a few spots. Trout
have both color and pattern variation.

These shells are all from the same
kind of scallop. What kind of
variation can you see?

Here is a garden with pansies.
Do you see any variation?

# Variation Review

1. Name five variations you can observe in people.

2. Tell about variation in trout.

3. Think of another animal, and tell about variation.

# Insect Shapes and Colors

Insects are different shapes and colors.
The shape or color can help an insect hide.
Then, an enemy cannot see it.
A hungry bird or lizard may think
these insects are thorns.

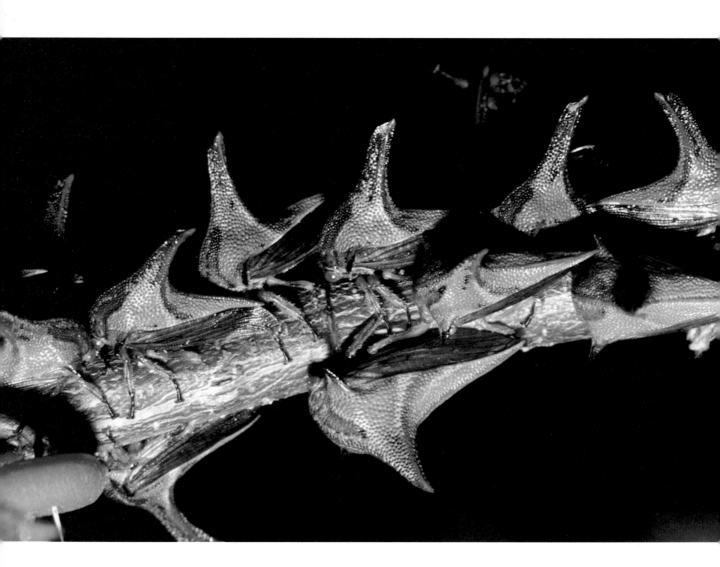

This leaf insect looks just like the leaves around it.

A walking stick on a twig is very hard to see. Can you find it?

Look at the bright colors and design on this
butterfly. Do you think it is hidden from
its enemies?

Some insects are very easy to see.
They are very colorful.
They may have special markings.

Brightly colored
insects often taste
bad. They make
other animals sick.
Animals learn to
stay away!

The spots on this beetle
look like huge eyes.
A hungry animal might
think the beetle is a
lot bigger. The animal
might be scared away.

# What Makes an Insect an Insect?

How can you tell if a creature is an insect? All insects have three body parts. These are the head, thorax, and abdomen. Insects also have six legs.

Most insects have one pair of antennae and one or two pairs of wings.

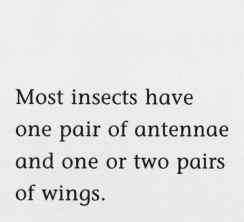

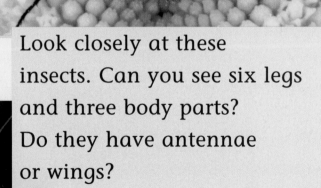

Look closely at these insects. Can you see six legs and three body parts? Do they have antennae or wings?

Some creatures look like insects,
but they are not. Which of these
are insects? How can you tell?

# What Makes an Insect an Insect?
## Review

1. What are the three body parts of an insect?

2. Tell about insect legs, antennae, and wings.

# Same but Different

Insects are alike in many ways. They have three body parts and three pairs of legs. Many have antennae and wings and hatch from **eggs.** But insects can look very different. Some have...

• antennae that look like feathers,

• long, long legs for jumping high,

- huge wings for flying far,

- beautiful colors and designs.

On land and in water,
under the ground
and high in the sky...
Insects are everywhere.
And they are amazing!

# Insect Life Cycles

Insects may look different at each stage of their lives. Most insects go through four stages. The stages are egg, **larva**, **pupa**, and adult. The eggs of this insect were laid inside cells.

After a couple of days, each egg hatches into a larva. The tiny larva stays curled up inside the cell. The larva eats food made from pollen and honey. This food makes the larva grow.

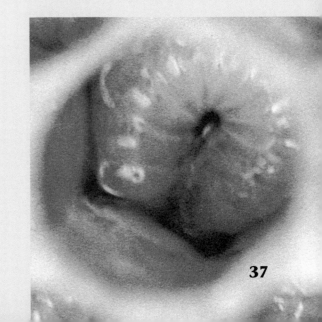

Then, the cell is covered with wax.
Inside the cell, each larva turns into a pupa.

In the pupa stage, the insect goes through a
big change. Soon, an adult crawls out of
each cell. Do you know what insect this is?

It's a bee! After a short rest, the bee can go right to work. Young adult bees work in the hive. Older bees work outside.

The larvae of different insects do not look the same. These larvae will become insects you know well. What will they look like as adults?

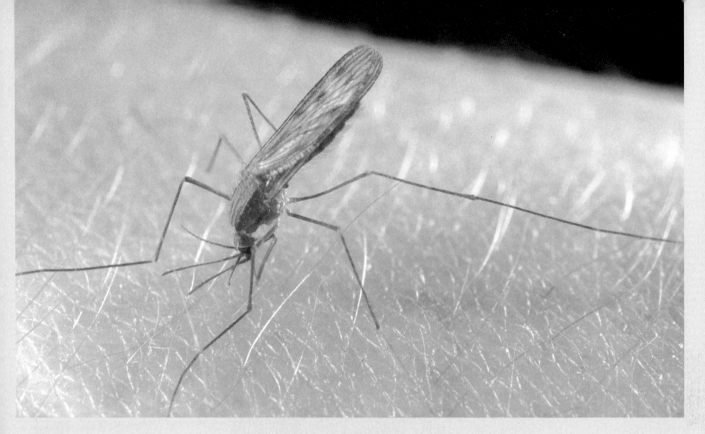

Mosquitoes...

and moths!

Some kinds of insects don't have larvae or pupae. When they hatch from their eggs, they are called **nymphs.** Many nymphs look a lot like the parents, but smaller.

Milkweed bugs go through about four nymph stages. In each new stage, they look a little more like an adult.

How many different nymph stages can you find?

# Insect Life Cycles Review

1. Tell about the life cycle of a bee.

2. Tell about the life cycle of a milkweed bug.

43

# Life Goes Around

On a lucky day, you might see a ladybug. It is red with black spots. It is an adult ladybug. But have you ever seen a baby ladybug?

Adult ladybugs mate. Then the female lays eggs. When an egg hatches, a larva comes out. The black larva is the baby ladybug. But it doesn't look like its parents. The larva eats and grows for three or four weeks.

Then it **pupates.** Inside the pupa, the larva is changing. When the pupa opens, an adult ladybug comes out. It is red with black spots. It looks just like its parents.

Some animals are born alive. Some animals hatch from eggs. They all grow up to be adults. The adults mate and reproduce babies called offspring. This is called a life cycle.

Cycle means to go around. Every animal goes around the life cycle. The life cycle of a ladybug looks like this.

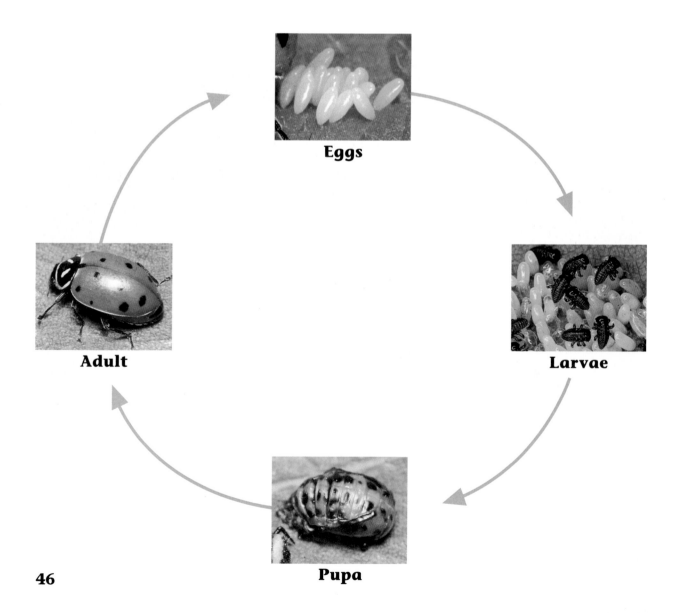

Eggs

Larvae

Pupa

Adult

The ladybug life cycle is like the life cycle of many other insects. It's like the life cycle of the mealworm. It's like the life cycle of butterflies and moths. But it is different from the life cycle of some other animals.

Trout lay eggs in streams. After six to eight weeks, the eggs hatch. Tiny, fat babies swim out. You can see that they are fish. But they don't look like their parents yet.

For the next year, they grow up little by little. In two years, they are adults. They look just like their parents. They mate and lay eggs in the stream. Can you describe the trout life cycle?

Frogs lay eggs in water, too. When an egg hatches, a tadpole swims out. It looks more like a fish with a big head than a frog. It doesn't look like its parents yet.

The tadpole eats and grows. In a few weeks, the tadpole starts to change. Its long flat tail gets shorter. Its legs start to grow.

In a few more weeks, the tadpole has grown into a frog. It looks just like its parents. Can you describe the frog life cycle?

Ducks lay eggs in a nest in a **marsh.** The mother duck sits on the eggs to keep them warm. When they hatch, the babies are fluffy and yellow. The babies are called ducklings. You can see that they are ducks, but they don't look like their parents yet.

The ducklings eat and grow. In a few weeks, they get their brown feathers. In a few months, they are grown up. They look just like their parents. In the next year, the grown-up ducks will mate. They will raise new families of ducklings. Can you describe the duck life cycle?

Mice do not lay eggs. Baby mice grow inside the mother. The babies are born alive. Newborn mice are pink, hairless, and blind. You can see that they are mice, but they don't look like their parents yet.

In a few days, the babies open their eyes. Their fur starts to grow. Mice grow up fast. In a few months, they will be adults. They will be ready to continue the life cycle and have babies of their own. Can you describe the mouse life cycle?

# Life Goes Around Review

1. Does the ladybug larva look like its parents?

2. Tell about the life cycle of a ladybug.

3. Tell about the life cycle of a different animal.

4. Name five animals that hatch from eggs.

5. Name some animals that are born alive (not as eggs).

# Glossary

**adult**   a fully grown organism. The last stage of a life cycle.

**antennae**   the long, thin "feelers" on the head of an insect.

**characteristic**   a feature of an animal or plant that you can observe.

**egg**   the first stage of a life cycle.

**environment**   the surroundings of a plant or animal.

**flower**   a part of a plant that grows into fruit in plant reproduction.

**fruit**   a part of a plant that has seeds in it. Flowers grow into fruit and fruit produce seeds in plant reproduction.

**inherit**   to get characteristics from parents.

**insect**   an animal that has six legs and three body parts. The three parts are the head, thorax, and abdomen. Most insects have antennae and wings.

**insect life cycle**   the stages in the life of an insect.  There are two kinds of insect life cycles. Some insects go through four stages (egg, larva, pupa, and adult). Other insects go from eggs to nymphs to adults.

**larva**   the form of an insect that hatches from eggs. The second stage in a life cycle. Insect larvae look different from their parents, often worm-like.

**life cycle**   the stages in the life of a plant or animal.

**marsh**   soft, wet land that is sometimes covered with water.

**nymph**   a stage in a life cycle of an insect where there is no larva or pupa. Nymphs look a lot like their parents, but smaller.

**offspring**   a new plant or animal produced by a parent.

**organism**   a living thing.  Plants and animals are organisms.

**pupa**   the form of an insect between the larva and adult stages. The third stage of a life cycle.

**pupate**   to change into a pupa.

**reproduction**   the process of producing offspring. Offspring are new plants or animals.

**seed**   a part of a plant formed in the flower and found inside fruit.  Seeds grow into new plants.

**variation**   a difference.

# Index